The Kinship of Ordinary Things
and Other Poems

The Kinship of Ordinary Things
and Other Poems

By
TODD OUTCALT

RESOURCE *Publications* • Eugene, Oregon

THE KINSHIP OF ORDINARY THINGS AND OTHER POEMS

Copyright © 2022 Todd Outcalt. All rights reserved. Except for brief quotations in critical publications or reviews, no part of this book may be reproduced in any manner without prior written permission from the publisher. Write: Permissions, Wipf and Stock Publishers, 199 W. 8th Ave., Suite 3, Eugene, OR 97401.

Resource Publications
An Imprint of Wipf and Stock Publishers
199 W. 8th Ave., Suite 3
Eugene, OR 97401

www.wipfandstock.com

PAPERBACK ISBN: 978-1-6667-6253-2
HARDCOVER ISBN: 978-1-6667-6254-9
EBOOK ISBN: 978-1-6667-6255-6

VERSION NUMBER 111522

To Becky, yet again

Contents

Sunrise Walk | 1
Venice in the Rain | 2
Forgiveness | 3
Art in Florence | 4
Homecoming | 5
Singing the Blues | 6
Young & Old Love | 7
The Kinship of Ordinary Things | 8
Hemingway's Home | 9
Among Paul Tillich's Ashes | 10
Camino de Santiago | 11
In Paris | 12
Description by the Blind | 13
Absolute Zero | 14
Plurals | 15
Horned Owl | 16
Gibbous | 17
Doodling | 18
The Indefatigable Memory of Light | 19
Why His Heart Breaks in Venice | 20
Everything Happens for a Reason | 21
Sexual vs. Sensual | 22
Seven Ways of Looking at a Nude Woman | 23
Garlic | 25
Contemplating Menopause | 26
Mona Lisa in the Louvre | 27

Painting the Nude | 29
The Church Bells at Noon | 30
One Woman Man | 31
The Misery of Stars | 32
James Merrill at the Ouija Board | 33
Gideon Bible | 34
The MorningNewspaper | 35
Anemone | 36
Coyote | 37
Sink | 38
Quatrains on Orgasm | 39
Sex Poem | 40
Black Not Me | 41
Painting a Canvas | 42
Speaking for the Dead | 43
Harvest | 44
Eustace Tilley | 45
Class Photos | 46
Antiques | 47
A Tree the Memory of a Tree | 48
Passenger Pigeons | 49
Waapaahsiki Siipiiwi Mound | 50
Making Coffee | 51
Medicine Cabinet | 52
Galileo's Finger | 53
Pat Down | 54
Grand Central Station | 55
The Circle of Father and Son | 56
When Not In Rome | 57
Arrival | 58
Interview: Cooking Chili | 59

Transference | 60
Acknowledgements | 61
Thaw | 62
Pandemic Prayer | 63
Unspoken Prayer | 64
Because of a Woman | 65
Sonnet Written at Noon, May Two | 66
Somnambulisms of Wine | 67
Wine Cellar | 68
Colloquy | 69
This is What It Will Be Like | 70
The Academy of Indigo | 71
Pomp & Circumstance | 72
June Psalm | 73
The Wasted Day | 74
Obituaries of Summer | 75
Kingdom Come | 76
Ageing | 77
The Sommelier in Winter | 78
Waking Among the Sequoias | 79
Homecoming | 80
The Tiny House | 81
An Evening Prayer | 82
McDonalds | 83

Acknowledgments | 84
About the Author | 85

Sunrise Walk

Strolling the streets with coffee in hand
I see your town and its tenements
Where some of my own thoughts rise
Like fog to meet the yellow eyes
Of blinded windows
And early alarms

I could pace across this vaulted landscape
For days and not exhaust the wanderlust
Of reason or the purple skies
Or hold in tension the hidden cries
Bonded with beauty
In a new day's charms

Why something else rises other than pain
Is a mystery only the butcher knows
Or cherished in the hands of the nurse
Leaving the hospital after a worse case
Scenario has lifted
Hope again

Somewhere in these streets I too revive
At the thought of a most remarkable
Brilliant sunrise coursing through the veins
Of distant people singing the refrains
Of other voices
Yet so glad to be alive

Venice in the Rain

I have always been thankful for the small things
Which seem to avail themselves to us
In fortuitous moments, rapturous wings,
Or the minutia of the serendipitous
Marvels on which our love clings:
A ledge perhaps or vacancy sign,
A light turned on to pave the dark,
A poor kid selling ponchos, a found dime
While drenched in a rainstorm that would float an ark.
And those blind alleys past the Rialto Bridge
Where we ran for cover, past our prime,
And found a restaurant, not privilege
Really, but in the nick of time
So reminiscent of all we've made of love.

Forgiveness

Every boy has a memory
Of the one that got away
As is the case with me
When I fished waters alone
On summer mornings
And made my way
Along familiar paths
To ponds that were then
Brightened by the early
Mists of May

The bass that leapt
And spit my line
So hard I later stood
Upon the bank and cried
To think it was so big
With promise

I'm ready now to cast again
Aged by wisdom
And all the dark time
That has passed between us
I am a child of the land
Eager to take to water
To let go of all that pain
That I felt then
And which I still don't understand

Art in Florence

Looking back I could have written
A thousand observations on the wind
Or David's song or the absolution
Of the vistas that we marveled
Over in their broad tapestries
Above the caramel-colored glen

I could have said *I love you*
As we strode the garden paths
Or made our way down the stone stairs
To the river road that seemed a bit
Too melancholy or like something
Of an ending now that I think of it

Or I could have kissed you on the bridge
As we stood there drenched in sun
Staring upward into that rise
Where we had once stood
Holding Florence in our hearts
And her gold reflection in your eyes

Homecoming

I went home again and walked those paths
I once had known—now so narrow
And so small. The fence lines draped
In clover ringed by vine.
There were tombstones on the hill
And where the trees grew tall
There stood a sense of time.

I could have worked there in the boyhood
Fields forever—or so it seemed.
But all the light had faded
From my mind, and there was only
Forward left to live. Some had passed
Or would pass away again. And then
Awhile I wanted to return in kind,
But knew I could not, nor would this last:
Leaving again what I
Had already left behind.

Singing the Blues

There is energy in sadness
That makes life tolerable in tears
Some moral sense of madness
That dispels those fears
Attributed to happiness

Most of us don't trust
Our good luck to hold much longer
So we smile and sing the blues
It's the crying makes us stronger
Or perhaps the joy of staring down
At the rhythm of our blue-sued shoes

Young & Old Love

Young love is all the rage
Wild horses streaking across a plain
Open-mouth kisses in the rain
Blue words on a page

But old love
Is never taken for granted
It is a fine wine decanted
The last of

A rare property with frontage
View of a calm sea
An apostrophe
Of youth in an antique age

Old love plays same suits
No games of pretense
A sure defense
No substitutes

Young love hyperventilates
But old love grays
Survives dark days
Hibernates

Old love lasts through young love's lies
A test of time
In pantomime
Of young love's face through old love's eyes

The Kinship of Ordinary Things

One day you will be at home
Reading a book perhaps
Or sorting laundry at midnight
When a friend may call with a dilemma
Or ask your advice with a problem

And one word will lead to another
There in the kinship of ordinary things
In the aroma of fresh-brewed coffee
Or the sweetness of freshly-folded towels
Where love meets at these intersections

This is of course the true course
From which all of life springs
And from which our sadnesses gift
The world with inexpressible joy
And into which we are baptized

Only let us seek them out as one
Prepared for the inevitable grace
Of quiet walks or the mirror image
Of our solitary talks through which
God grants his favor in another's face

Hemingway's Home

Key West, 2016

There were always palm trees peering out onto the Atlantic
And even then the six-toed cats shitting in the courtyard
Beneath the writing loft
Mornings productive before sunrise when the mind was pure
Or the marlins would rise in the silver surf of vacant afternoons
As there were no bells tolling in the steeples
Nor unheralded safaris into the dark jungles of the mind

One might have heard the *rat-a-tatting* of the Remington
Or the *tinkling* of ice in bourbon glasses
Exploring the distances between calamitous loves
Or perhaps the snow-capped mountains gazing down upon
Blue waters or the raucous collision of Wallace Stevens
Where the gray days of inebriation first snatched looks
From the blank pages of beautifully unwritten books

Among Paul Tillich's Ashes

New Harmony, Indiana

There will always be an ultimate concern
Extracted from green varieties of gifts
Such as the cadences of cicadas
Or the trepidations of the clandestine owl
    Or one may find along the narrow path
    Congregations of the fiddlehead fern
    Underfoot like a cat on the prowl

Most of these could preach much louder
If we would give them their due
Or dredge from their surreptitious meekness
    A bold language unexpressed through word
    Or a place that one might misconstrue
    As a sanctuary from which could be heard
    A silent proclamation yet alltogether true

Camino de Santiago

Centuries have withstood the ecclesiastical force
Of the crypts or what became of the bones
Of the bones of other saints turned pilgrim
Where some pink-soled and starving arrived
Naked across the barren landscape of Galicia

Come kilometers with nothing but water in hand
Mourning the familiar prayers or wretched
In the trenches of their native land
These colonies of transubstantiated lovers
Spelled by the tintinnabulations of the cuckoo

What warms the hungry pilgrim is the length
Or what could be found in head and heart
As truth adored in that same bare place
Or discovered in the familiar face
That was left back home by that distant hearth

In Paris

We stride a wet Champs-Elysees
Embraced by rain, in love
With bread and every smiling face
That greets us at The Louvre.
The windows high in Sainte-Chapelle
Speak to us frame-by-frame,
As we are stirred by every bell
That rings from Notre Dame.
We kiss admiring the small flower
Of laughter like old friends,
In love beneath the Eifel Tower
Just like Parisians.

Description by the Blind

Some years ago I met a man on the street who was selling brooms
A blindness that had left him joyous in the dark and yet not bitter
But industrious in his occupation mastering the golden spin of straw

And for some reason I felt compelled to ask him to describe what he saw
Or could not see there in the street or where he lived in other rooms
And he reached down into his basket and brought this hither

I see what you see he said *but it is not as you see I'm sure*
As what I see is of one luxurious color distinguished by particles of sound
Just as your voice is distinctive I see you as you are

But not as others see you which is neither better nor worse
What I see are heavenly textures which may sound bizarre
But no less strange to me than what you see here on the ground

Absolute Zero

Between stars those infinitesimal points of light
A cold fills the void unfueled by solar breezes
God's laboratory colder than the darkest night
The pendulum where all molecular movement ceases
And some are living in this now though they are warm
In summer houses and tanned by southern yellow sun
Not knowing when the mercury may shatter or harm
Their supernova hanging by a megaton
And more in cryogenics have outlived their prime
Or frozen solid heart and mind and single soul
Peering into theories lost in Hawking's time
And wondering if they lived where would they go

Plurals

When words bloom in language
A bag becomes *baggage*,
A *fungus, fungi,*
Syllabus, syllabi.
Some words are unchanged: like *species* or *sheep*.
While few like *plateaux* are imponderably deep.

And words like *oases*
Might cover the *bases*
Or *splashes* and *dashes*
Parlayed for *neuroses.*
But no one refuses their *sheaves* for a sheaf
Though some might confuse their *beliefs* for belief.

The multiplication
Of *station* or *nation*
Is not *sons-in-law*
Numbered in *chateaux,*
But nouns dropped in speech like so many *feces*
Demand plural rules and multiple *theses.*

Horned Owl

One afternoon while standing at the kitchen window
I sensed the shadow of a giant wing
Which draped its mass upon a limb
And there in sunlight was the brilliant owl
Its hooded face a dark and brooding thing
With petal feathers soft and dancing in the wind

It stared at me with coal black eyes as if to say
I do not fear the predator that comes in light
An understanding that we shared however brief
The miracle that two of us should meet by day
Or having heard its question in my night
To watch its flight and grieve it on its way

Gibbous

A portion missing
Is greater than the whole
As one can see the contour
Of distance divided
On the surface late in June

Though if romance is insisting
In a vacuum like a bowl
One might part that door
And declare love's light
From the dark side of the moon

Doodling

Consider the triangles, the curlicues,
The trapezoid houses brick-by-brick,
The one-eared dog chasing his big stick
As you talk on the telephone overhearing the news . . .
    Of a death perhaps or homicide,
    Or phone the pizza order in—
    Waiting for someone to listen
    To your explanation before they decide
To cancel your insurance or sell your stock.
That's why you draw the perfect square:
To see if you can find yourself there
In that ball of hair, that grandfather clock,
    Or if that curl of smoke is hiding a flame
    That could consume you, frame by frame.

The Indefatigable Memory of Light

Sometimes he returns to himself as a boy
Remembering such soiled days as the planting
Or the harvest consumed by crows.
He does not understand his younger joy
Nor if the earth is the sound of his singing
Though these are the songs he knows.

Often he follows himself through a twilight
Of lightening bugs or opens his hand
To touch his younger face as a star,
Or as he leans upon the distant love of night
He hastens even yet to that far land
Of memory that defines his dreams as they are.

And sometimes in his loneliness he returns
To the laughter of his childhood friends,
Finding solace in their common charm
Where some of his soul still burns—
A perfection of memory in triumphant ends,
His heart still warmed by what he never learns.

Why His Heart Breaks in Venice

These are the long shadows of the light on water
The pastel colors rising on the threatening sea
While in the alleys there are songs he cannot sing
And words he cannot speak through his soliloquy

What might he forfeit or what forces can he bring
To bear upon the life he knows is leaving
Having loved her long through his own centuries
Before he realized his heart was grieving

And on the bridges staring at the Pleiades
He waits to make a declaration at the end
While even in his passion he is weak of heart
But takes her hand that he might drown again

Everything Happens for a Reason

But suppose, Horatio, that the opposite is truth:
That *nothing* happens for a reason.
Suppose that stars collide in random fire,
That black holes eat time and matter indiscriminately,
That planets form, or not, in the dark rectum of space.

And suppose that on this floating orb we live and die
At the hands of fate and fools and molecules
That collide in no apparent order or desire.
One might arrive at other conclusions instead of cliché,
Or seek other explanations through something higher.

And suppose that in this randomness we pass this way
But once and must learn to make the best of it.
Or that even here we discover life's sacred worth
In the freedoms where we choose to live and hope,
Embracing love even while proclaiming *that's all she wrote.*

Sexual vs. Sensual

She was asking about the difference
Between sexual and sensual
Suggesting I thought a compromise
Between the two
      And I pointed out that light
      Was particle and wave at once
      And for illustration
      Pointed at the full moon

Seven Ways of Looking at a Nude Woman

I
He thinks if there had been more wine in the mix
Some of his conversation would have been funny
And may have led to sex

II
A man can never be certain she is not a mantis
But is most grateful for having survived the coitus
Without losing his head

III
He is not thinking about sex at all but about how
In the perfect Platonian plane she is a rare combination
Of body mind and soul

IV
Of course he is thinking about sex
Which happens about every seven minutes on average
And is also about how long it lasts

V
The moon is perfect much like her breasts
And the way her hands move against
The silk roadmap of her skin

VI
He is a visual creature which is why she is nude
As she leans over the bathroom sink
To brush her teeth

VII
He wants to express his love in ways other than this
Not just looking at her that way but in every other way
That does not lead to a kiss

Garlic

It grows in bulbs like flowers parsed in pauses
Small bullets shooting their lead in concupiscent crèmes
Each clove far more potent that it seems
Or stirred in pastas unrepentant in their respective sauces

Contemplating Menopause

Men wonder how they escaped so great a change
In the blood, their mouths still yearning for the salt,
Their bodies lank in fits of age, the strange
Mannerisms of their wives a gestalt
That they have nourished in murky mystery.
Men often ponder how such strength resides
In estrogen. They mark the perigee
Of the moon, the last month's fratricides,
Guilty of the basest thoughts. Her eyes
Are no more fixed on his but flood with tears
At slightest moods. He does not want to beg
For the limp biscuit in his final years,
Nor admit what his own heart belies:
That he is mourning for her final egg.

Mona Lisa in the Louvre

We wait in line
    We do our time
        By centimeters move
Humanity
    That's come to see
        The Mona Lisa in the Louvre

You feel the pinch
    As inch-by-inch
        The line snakes in a groove
Dreaming awhile
    You smile her smile
        Like Mona Lisa in the Louvre

Then at the last
    You hasten past
        Great works of art and prove
That you don't care
    What else is there
        But Mona Lisa in the Louvre

One final push
    And then you rush
        A chaos in commove
To glimpse in mass
    Da Vinci's caste
        His Mona Lisa in the Louvre

Yes there is art

    Back at the start
        But none of them behoove
The hours of wait
    Right from the gate
        As Mona Lisa in the Louvre

Painting the Nude

The idea of art is the act of an idea
Fleshed out in pigment
Or perhaps the keeper of time
A mere abstraction

The body is the result of an idea
Brushed in brown to pink
An abdication to the thrones
Of irony as one might think

Of a body outside a body
As subject matter
The torsos no less fatter
Than Ruben dreamed in ink

The Church Bells at Noon

They say the old ways are still among us
As the spirit of song, as robed innocence,
The vested priests open for confession,

The choirs thinned in the long arms
Of literalism, the loss of metaphor.
Augustine gone—Jerome and Origen, no more.

But the voice of the waters ringing
Distills the creed, the transubstantiation,
The hymns believed in one voice singing.

There is nothing left to learn,
No time for error, all change is sin,
And mere beliefs where faith has fled to burn again.

One Woman Man

Let me say on this unpretentious evening
Drowned in transcendence of candlelight
What a man cannot confess in light of day
Nor the wind disease in his airy throat
All the words in his resume

But that you have redeemed in varied hue
Those colors we have lived in fact
Extracted through some grand design
Or painted blank on canvass whole
Proclaimed as sibylline

The broken pieces of respective lives
Or what I could not mend for you
Though this has proved enough for me
To hold you here and punctuate our love
With this apostrophe

The Misery of Stars

At the rim of the universe
The fire
Has already burned out of them
Their bodies stone
Cold red
Their lights dim

They are just now
Reaching earth
With their supernova deaths
Touching us
With the history
Of their respective births

We can't see their misery
Through the haze
Of the Milky Way
But feel them staring at us
Through our dome of sleep
Like holes punched in papier-mache

James Merrill at the Ouija Board

Were there traces of fingers, voices that you heard?
Or were the letters drawn like chalk marks on the page?
Please tell us "The Changing Light at Sandover"
Was like a bird in flight, a beautiful ossifrage
That winged over your spirit or the spirits of the dead.
Or let us believe what you believed in those years
When Jackson filled the lines, when the cold thread
Of your heart was buried in that length of work.
There were, of course, reprisals—gaudy destriers
Galloping across the board in Auden's hand,
Or perhaps those ancient histories that would shirk
The page, of coming forth to speak in cryptonym.
You rode across that plain, that solitary land—
A poet Jew, lost in the voice of Ephraim.

Gideon Bible

I have been on the road for a long time
Bored out of old suitcases and wrinkled clothes
Wary of the cum-covered sheets
And flashing neon signs burning the windows

The only consistency in the drawer by the bed
Is always there by the phone book
Where they tell me red light hookers have found the Lord
Or sometimes traveling salesmen
Eager for a one night stand
One nation under God world without end amen

I have read the whole but never in bed
Preferring instead the comfort of familiar lips
Or a good book by Stephen King
I love the Lord but I love to shed
The weight of holy habits
Especially when she is willing to do a new thing

The MorningNewspaper

I continue to continue to seek the lost
To redeem the bundle curbside
With more than a modicum of excitement

This daily artifact of dinosaur bones
My children have never unearthed
My toast and coffee an exhibit to their snide

Remarks saying I am a fossil myself
Pinching the tender grit of ink
Between my blackened fingers

I collect the rubber bands on a shelf
Though page by page I think
I see the ancient extinctions still among us

Though my histories will not return
From dust to complete the crossword puzzle
Or laugh their comic wit with me

But reading this old excitement
I pause to wonder if I might
Be too far gone or too contrary

To read my own obituary
Or even to see my future evolution
Recorded in the wonder of fine print

Anemone

Brilliant red, translucent pea,
A much-maligned floral debris,
It clings and springs like a bungee
Cord from any key—
Siesta, West, or blue Capri—
The anemone.

And fish, some of them amputee,
Are not released from its esprit.
Its tentacles much like a tree
Whose limbs reach out, a devotee
Of caviar and filigree—
The anemone.

Its welcome, like a maitre d',
Is refuge to the refugee
Who find such poisons disagree-
Able to any pedigree
That swims into that deadly sea
Of the anemone.

Coyote

The animal in the night is a mentality
That cannot assuage the bestial water
While clenching the weight of light in its silver teeth
But there is a beauty in the bestiality
Of the hunt for the muskrat and the otter
And joy in the blood that lies beneath

Nowhere is the moon shedding its light
To help the cold and hungry dog to sleep
Free of the clutch of its poverty
But the horned owl flies above the night
Sinking its thorny talons into the deep
Fleshpots of the underbelly we cannot see
While the pack is running the stirrup of the creek
Howling in the heart and preying on the weak

Sink

It was there—this ancient thing—
When I checked into my room
And slouched on the edge of the bed.
But later, I noticed its dull ring
When I was brushing my teeth soon
After my evening meal. It said:

"I have lived many lives here
Below the mirror, as soiled hands
Have touched my knobs, or felt
The silk of water or the sheer
Pleasure of clean. One understands
By water how a life is dealt.

And you are touching dirt
That has passed through centuries
Of sin—that same whore
Who was fucked up her skirt,
Or the cum on the sheets,
Washed here wanting more.

But do not judge me harsh
As you stand over my bowl
Or consider me just a sink.
I am here, willing to let you wash
Away your sins, be made whole,
And I, much cleaner than you think."

Quatrains on Orgasm

Each one has its own language, a place
And time that could be remembered for
Insignificant dramas, conversations,
A modicum of aroma, color, décor.

Some speak the word of quick release,
The loss of senses or the piquing of—
While others drive a hard bargain and cannot
Be coerced except by the voice of love.

Some are poems still being written,
Play with words, not yet complete—
A vice that is squeezing tighter
Aching for denouement or the quick release.

Some are sermons that drill the core
Of ancient sorrows, horrors, ploys—
Bereaving the spirit while the body is sore
From prolonged redemption through its joys.

And some are pure and simply lust
That none can master over pains—
Call it depraved or sin if you must,
But sex is the master and love the chains.

Sex Poem

One doesn't always set out to write a poem about sex
Or the slow joy of weightless being in that moment
One is released from the incarcerated self
Unless this is more difficult to procure than wine
Less common than lusting for wealth
Or cannot be achieved in time

Nor does one ponder the significance of sex
As a selfless act as it is the discovery of soul
To see the other as one might know one's self
The splitting of the atom
Or the renting of complex parts
Before the two are made one whole

Black Not Me

I see the world through white eyes
Unsuspecting of flags and tags and hoods
Which will come as no surprise
To those who have understood
The long thread of race like a filament
That has leavened our daily bread
As no one asks what I meant
By my smile or what I said

Nor few if any will find fault
With the pale side of my sickly skin
Or ponder if my intellect
Is as pure as my gestalt
Or if the judgment that casts me out
Is greater than the crimes that let me in

Painting a Canvas

The key is beginning which is the prime mover
As often I think of your colors pleasing you
Even in the dark. A man cannot explain such things
But hold to them on the palate lifting the brush.

I am not creating the end as one might know a lover
But all that is left of me will no longer misconstrue
This art for even the commonest of things
Or may offer you illimitable beauty
As I paint for love while all about me sings.

Speaking for the Dead

Another Eulogy for remembering
That we are not forgotten
And even in the forest for the trees
We can find the one true thing
Such as the way he drew a breath
Or how she without brushes
Painted the last supper of lasagna

Some will then discover
In the far country of despair
That death is the beautiful cloud
Or the horrendous fire that lights the night
Not so unlike the joy of the swallow
Or the magnificent music of life
Before it draws its last gasp of air

Harvest

Driving late to an appointment
I stopped along the road to watch
The harvest coming in
The giant combines combing
Yellowed fields of corn
And for a moment
I was reborn in memories
Of a father's love and hands
That toiled the fields
Work never done

High above me the autumn sun
Tossed down a smile
And nothing in my life gleaned
More important than that one
Bright moment there
I was going nowhere after all
Content to witness the river of grain
Flowing into that polished bin
Knowing nothing would come of my life
Except the joy of planting it again

Eustace Tilley

Sometimes he's somber, sometimes silly,
Collar up, austere and frilly.
A gentleman of sorts, though nearly
Common to the touch, but clearly
Content to observe a chilly
Distance from the facts, though really
He's a Ross's man so neatly
Drawn in character, his lily
Face a name, a single-mini
Literati: *Eustace Tilley*.

Class Photos

Some refuse to return from the dead
While others flame as unrequited love
Not all the teachers remembered by name

The one girl tanned in summer dress instead
Of bell-bottom jeans is now dreaming of
Retirement and cashing in her 401-K

The captain of the football team
Is bald and fat and imperially gray
As are his legions cutting down their nets

And the loose girl every boy's dream
Is a four-time grandma on her way
To condo in Florida before she forgets

How young we were and promising
In those simple years of dance
When all our dreams were high as air

Implied as we stood our smiling rows to sing
In ignorance of some high romance
And of the Kodachrome which binds us there

Antiques

If one stares deeply enough into the centuries
The ghosts return to dine at table
Or sit in wicker rocking chairs to sew

Even the portraits gaze back in realities
Rich with mink or black sable
Dead long before their smiles could grow

The tiny tins and brittle toys
No longer hold their promise rusted out
The clocks unwound no longer chime

But we see in those photos the girls and boys
We used to know though we will doubt
Ours will fade like them or run out of time

A Tree the Memory of a Tree

They grew tall once as oak and sycamore
The pines egregious as any sin
None so old as the redwoods before
The Spanish arrived in their legion
Of pox to fell the cathedrals of ash

Only the eldest eyes could see
Through smoke and mirror to glimpse the stars
Their silver portents a mystery
Comforting the lost tribes dim powers
Exchanged for beads and promises

Some would know centuries before
That the forests would disappear
From the foundations of the earth's floor
Vacant as the sky that binds us here

Passenger Pigeons

Once their numbers eclipsed the sun
When they flew by millions from field to field
The light gone out of them sported and killed
Great swarms of them falling to earth by the ton
How their blue feathers made a meal for hogs
Or could anyone seen their oblivion on the horizon
Blown bright pink at the barrel of a gun
Their extinction as easy as falling off logs
The last one at the Cincinnati Zoo
Martha was a spectacle of death
Betraying her millions in her final breath
Her fame higher than any bird ever flew
A century later not even her distant squab
Could die in numbers large enough to be macabre

Waapaahsiki Siipiiwi Mound

Fairbanks, Indiana—July 2015

Centuries before the river died and parted
The squaws carried baskets of black earth
To the crest of the mound
And danced before the new moon
Light from light mixed with clay
Sparks rising from the ancestral fire

But see how the ash has grown
And the oak stretched toward the sun
As if the elders are still speaking
To the great company
Their arms lifted now in the land
Of the remembered

Making Coffee

One brews the ritual first
The time of rising
Brushing teeth
The water poured
The filtering
To quench the thirst

Then to bequeath
The anticipation
Of the blackened bean
Found in the first rush
Flush with the elation
Of caffeine

Medicine Cabinet

After his death we retrieved
The artifacts of his-story:
Pills he had grieved
Through nearly a century,

Vials of Carter's little pills,
Cod liver oil that seemed
To heal all ills,
A tube of Brylcreem

Still in its thick shape,
Prescriptions seized
Or long past date
Of their potencies,

Poly-dent paste,
Old Spice cologne
Splattered in haste
After shaving alone

When last he used
Nitroglycerin or
A finger of booze
To ease before

His heart gave out
From his medical ruse.
Dead no doubt
Despite his use.

Galileo's Finger

In a small glass dome
Florence, Italy
You can see it still
Poised and eager
For the truth

The astronomer's finger
Leathered onyx brown
Displayed amid
His artifacts
And charged offenses

A piece of him yet
Witnessing to the triumph
Of science
As if having left gravity
As he found it

Or perhaps writing
In bone and flesh
Of eternity
While still pointing
At the stars

Pat Down

Leaving Guatemala I am among five
Selected at random for strip and cavity search
My palms and crotch swabbed
By unsmiling airport authority

I consider the residues of my last adventure
Oil of corn tortilla juice of lime
Fingerprints of gentle people
The barley hops of the warm beer

What they are looking for
Is the worst part of me
Hoping that I will leave myself behind
Like traces of inebriation

I give them nothing in the end
And so they zip me up and send
Me off into the wild blue darkness of night
"Adios, Amigo. Have a nice flight."

Grand Central Station

So many conjunctions all converging here
Some of them going nowhere

From the balconies it is evident they have come
Pakistani Greek Italian French Saudi Swede

Laying tracks across the Atlantic
Bridging the center to an island so much to see

Or upon dreaming at last of home
A final bagel and cream cheese

Digesting bits of America or
Holding on to a forgotten hope they cannot leave

The Circle of Father and Son

What is a father to do when he can no longer remember his son?
The way the football spiraled through the air, the lilt of laughter,
The moments when the big games were lost or won?

How can a father make his son remember the good times if there were none,
Or that is how the son remembers his life or the father's love?
How can a father return to bless a memory or create a new outcome?

What is a son to do if he can no longer remember his father as one
Of his heroes, or honor the father as the memory of a friend?
What if the son leaves his father, or decides that he will shun

All of the shared history or forget the races they used to run?
How can a father fill the vacancies of a distant son
When he has fled and lost the memory of love or when it first begun?

When Not In Rome

This is the poem I did not write to you
When we dined late on the Seine
And kissed by the market fountain
Near the Coliseum

All of the light gone blue on the bridge
Transfixed by the angel's wings
So let us linger here in these lines
Inviting love to stay

Arrival

—To Chelsey & Logan

At first there was only the anticipation
Of your coming, the hour a long way off,
And only the idea of you before we first laid eyes.

Your mother knew your moods, your heart,
And I was a quiet observer of your growth.
I had practiced our first hello before we said our last goodbyes.

Sometimes I would stir in the middle of the night
Dreaming you were on your way, but fall asleep
Again in the space of flesh between us where you kicked.

But the day of your arrival was choked with light,
And tears were brushed with triumph, you complete
With head and shoulders, knees and toes, all slicked.

It's difficult to know how we survived
Learning what we've learned since you arrived.

Interview: Cooking Chili

There's nothing better in this pot.
Shit, I can tell you that.
Dump in all the peppers you've got
Like rabbits into a hat.

I don't use a recipe.
Got it all in my head.
A pinch of cinnamon, a Bay leaf,
Bake corn bread,

Fry bacon, roast tomatoes, beans,
A dash of sugar to sweet.
Set the bowls out, spoons clean.
Let's eat.

Transference

The shaggy dogs of summer remind me of winter days
    As do the cherry trees in their decays
Or how in the illimitable beauty of red roses
I see evidence of your love or the moot
Majesty of the eagle as it reposes
Among the peach blossoms of autumn fruit
    I could address these metaphors
Or find their meaning through other doors

Or consider how we have notched in time
    The manner in which wisteria climbs
Upon the arbor and through it hear our ageing voices
Calling out to our youthful days ubiquitous
The bouquets of banquets or our slim choices
Never so disturbing to cause all that fuss
    As nothing in life proves so demur
As beauty disguised as provocateur

I could make a simile of everything
    If you were so inclined to sing
Of facts and fingers and children flown
Through our most auspicious atmosphere
Or perhaps content in all we've known
Except to say that God was here
    Where we transposed our lives' preview
Into a music . . . déjà vu

Acknowledgements

I would like to thank
the ubiquitous ink
without which nothing transposes
onto the page
which is a higher order
and to think
that even the sun supposes
no accomplishment
without its light

Of course I thank
my agent
and the kitchen sink
as these have by rank
and file spent
years making me
much clearer
than I think

And to my wife
I save
a final thanks
as I would
otherwise have
no life
nor even space
to put
these words in
their proper place

Thaw

Mid-February ice
Dances from limbs of oak
Translucent rice
Like teardrops soak

The front porch step
Revealing layered hues
Of winter left
In their scabbard shoes

And swift and tiny rivulets
Thread down the drain
Forming vignettes
Of spring again

Pandemic Prayer

Let me stand along and long upon the tower wall
Overlooking these uncertain cloistered days
And let me serve as more than watchful eyes
Let my hands be open and my feet be swift
To brave the unseen elements
In the smallest of things

Let the nurse sing and the doctor stand tall
Among the microscopic enemies
So that even the fearful fear of the coming grace
And let the angry succumb to the angelic face
Giving the tide pause
And the future wings

Unspoken Prayer

One does not dare to address the wonder
Of the iris or the cacophony of crows
Or presume to speak into the void
Of a wasted day where all one knows
Is watching clouds

They say the wind blows where it wills
Which is to say nothing in spite
Of the wild intrusion of human things
Which we have foisted onto the world
In their multitude

So silence is the one true friend
And nothing else to count on here
Where our beginnings flee before us
Even if nothing greater than our greatest fear
Greets us at the end

Only stand in awe as that is ample
Enough to be a person in this air
To watch the eagle fly toward nothingness
Or hold the lover's hand in grace
And let this be our prayer

Because of a Woman

The game was forfeited for the long drive home
The bed mussed the white wine poured
Which was the fastest route to children

The job was the dream of the mortgage
Which led to other desperate debts
Which led to laughter and quiet evenings

So that by attrition she alone was there
Excluding the dog the cat the bored
Expression at the top of the stair

Which led to no one going anywhere
Except to distant anniversaries
Or frozen meals on dirty plates

Or as they say in movies where
They grow old together year by year
They could not have foreseen this coming

Which led to the final riot acts
Or the pure enjoyment of ice cold beer
Among the memories clinging to their backs

Sonnet Written at Noon, May Two

Softly the morning rain drifted away
In tribulations of the heart, mere fragments
Fragmenting into fragrances of lilac and mown grass,
The day awakening to white and primrose blue.
    Nothing to the point would make it last
    Or keep the faith from folding into spring decay,
    Jump on the bandwagon to see it through.

There were metaphors in conjunctions of gray,
Tucked into threats, folded into promises of reciprocity,
Books strewn among the half-completed essays of the past.
    The sirens stirred the languid air like a vast sea
    And all at once the anachronisms had their say
    Apparent that these perjuries would not last
    Exposed as counterfeits of another day.

Somnambulisms of Wine

The vintner roams among the moonlit hills
Dreaming of the perfect vine

His hands brushing the trellises flush
With Pinot or the blood of Cabernet

He cannot sleep for fear of the harsh rain
Or the hot sun bored into his Chardonnay

So even his consciousness is seared
By history and his auspicious art

As he wipes the sweat from his wine
Or drifts darkly into cellars of the mind

Where a time he will live in oak-charred barrels
Or argue his claim to be Bordeaux

His old world redeemed by Beaujolais
Through dreams where nothing but vines can grow

Wine Cellar

The history of years—of lives and warfare—
Is stored here among the bottled sun
The inebriations of air
The granite quarries of the stars

Here one can placate the Phoenicians' portion
The Roman gods of vine
Caligula quaffing his goblets of blood
Jesus offering himself as wine

Or linger behind the tilted corks
In artifacts of vintages
That opened may reveal degrees
Of their elusive histories

Colloquy

Art for art's sake is the structure of genius
The ordered sequence of the mind
Which one may redeem slowly
In luminous hues that cannot be evaded

Or consider the savage in the academy
Lecturing on theories of parochial theme
Which have not in their profundity
Ever been tried

It is the creation of the thing itself that is being
Or being brought into being that is real
A temporal thing which one may touch in time
And through its being learn how to feel

This is What It Will Be Like

This is what it will be like
When luck turns over a new leaf
Or the rain subsides and the blue sky rules

It will be like a new sun rising
The primitive salute of some
Evocative silence without tone

Like hearing the rapturous echo
Of thunder on the notorious mountains
Or the familiar music of one voice

Some even the strings can play
When nothing can hold back the joy
Triumphant in that new day

The Academy of Indigo

Let the cave dweller write
In coal and red night
Scrawl across the dripping wall

Or the deep forest heart
Mark the spider's art
Captured tooth and nail

In clandestine shadows when
Under wraps hemmed in
By caliginous matter

A pall falls across the pit
Where the fears of the decrepit
Follow after

Pomp & Circumstance

Let us speak now of the graduations of the mind
The bassoons of flickering keys in sharps and flats
As nothing so enrages the parent as poetry
Or postulates the certitudes of guilty pleasures
Learned in back rows on silent afternoons

Yet gowns will flash in the cordial sum of gratitude
And the teachers bask in the glow of placated light
Even as the stadium empties its bowels of ineptitude
Or the climate change from faith to fear
Before the future is saluted or the world made right

June Psalm

Benedictions as they are in green pastures
Are hallowed for their name's sake
In the kingdom of June
While the will of celestial bodies
On earth as in heaven
Is the still water

There are portions overflowing like laughter
And more than enough cups
To comfort after
The right paths like roads walked
Through the dark valley following goodness
And mercy forever

The Wasted Day

The fact that he slept late had nothing to do
With the irony of the mown grass or the painted gate
Nor the iron will of reading books while the dead flies
Collected at the bottom of the window sill

Rather jocose were the dishes in the kitchen sink
As were the bright banjoes of the garden hose
Or the brushes distilling in brown jars of turpentine
Near the back door where the morning thrushes

Would often conflagrate to warp their chorus
And cause him to pause then hesitate
Over the unread paper which he had confirmed
As the reason for saving his lunch for later

Looking west he could ascertain the reason
Why God had made the day for rest

Obituaries of Summer

The birds have borne the word through brighter lights
Over oceans of innuendo to speak the insufferable truth
Of the turning leaf and the harvest moon

Although in memory the children have seen such sights
As the white sparkle of the water was the fruit
Of an August that passed away too soon

Kingdom Come

Now the phenomena of the osprey wing
And the shadows of the moon have spoken
To eulogize the dark syllables of the miracle
Which for centuries remained contingent
Upon the ossuaries of belief

Or consider how beauty has been transformed
From the migrations of prayer into the beneficence
Of the beetle or the rhythms of the sea
Or how the landscapes overshadow the songs
Once sung in the stone cathedrals

Or note how the order of chaos
And the evolution of summer rains
Have opened the musty books
To fashion a new faith from the haunting
Melodies of such familiar old refrains

Ageing

Hints and innuendoes do not arrive at once
Ranged along prescriptions of relief
But residually creep into the cells like sieves
Their witness indicative of the grief
That is to come
                The ultimate camouflage
Is embryo of the mind
                And youthfulness
Plays tricks on the body's entourage
And does not allow for wrinkles to confess
The sum of the parts or critique the absolute
Delinquency of the wilting eyes or veins
That lick the surface of the sanguine suit
Once pink but patched in loquacious refrains
By experts who must have their say
Denying the truth that life succumbs to gray

The Sommelier in Winter

Certain vintages will be remembered for their climb
Their high-marks or the raspberry tongue
While others sitting in their stems like peach
Will fall markedly out of time

A pallor may settle over the palate like snow
Or drift back from the cellar's cold
But the Pinot like Cab will have its spring
And open like a fine Bordeaux

All good things like June fruit
Will eventually return to their returning
Tastes recalled from the pocket of a suit
With the tongue still burning

Waking Among the Sequoias

Five hundred feet is a thousand years
In a tree's life. Yet high among the lichen
And the beetles' time flies in the tears
Of the sun an awakening of stars
Where a new day has begun.

But should the bough break and one fall
From such a great height there would orchestrate
A swarm of words, a distant call
Of ancient history that one might cull
Together as a means to contemplate

The long arcs of civilization
Or perhaps a sense of found fear,
An insignificance, a deprivation
Of one's place in the cosmos, discovered
At the summit of nature's chandelier.

Homecoming

The hardware store is gone, as is the pharmacy,
The five-and-dime. But the library remains
As the last bastion of hope since the plastics factory
Closed its vacant shell. Now, what sustains
The slim streets are the paths of wild flowers
Growing in abandoned lawns. The town hall
Is a bingo parlor for the Catholic church, and hours
After the doors close a silence, like a pall,
Settles over the grand marquis where we once sat
On car hoods and necked. The moon has risen
For the last time over the names we forgot.
But trains still rumble by on the rusty track
Reminding us how far we have come
And how long the greater distance back.

The Tiny House

There is always a husband and wife
Sometimes a red-headed child excited about sleeping in a loft
Which serves double-duty as a storage unit

A bathroom with a composting toilet
Sits next to a kitchen sink and gas burners
So that the family can mingle during meals

And folding shelves hunker under windows
Each of which opens to a world of possibilities
Such as a flower garden littered with lawn chairs

Or the majestic oaks which splay their branches
Of protection over a marginalia of larger dreams
Opening like the roof toward some hidden but distant sun

An Evening Prayer

On this night of consternation and sighs
Let me recall with purpose the pastiche
Of praise and pain that graced these meetings
In the hurried solitude of a hundred greetings
That were in fact epiphanies
In a crowded life

Let me hold in tension the morning's coffee
And the evening's glass of cabernet
Even as I recount the arguments
That held sway over the soiled accoutrements
Of a weary world
And another day's decay

As though recalling a momentary slight
For what was said or not credited to my account
I give now nothing in return for what is mine
Except small antidotes of sorrow that entwine
The mornings' proclamations
With the silent night

And should I fail to mention in their magnitude
The small acts or kindnesses looming
Within these difficulties and their keep
Unwind in me some bothersome relief
A gratitude blooming
Among the bright flowers of sleep

McDonalds

There was a time when I studied the menu
Before ordering, as if the world had changed
Overnight and left me wanting more.
But now I am loving the people here
And wondering where these travelers,
With their five children and the Labrador,
Are headed? What brought them here
To these golden arches near the exit ramp
On their way to God-knows-where?
I could make a study of the man
Wearing the plaid shirt and greasy tie.
Or I could wonder (if I wondered *why*)
How a child could eat four burgers
In one sitting, including fries.
Being here, I am honored to be among
This brave band of pilgrims
Who have not yet figured out how we
Fit into one small car.
But I am miles from home and I smile
Every once and a while, grateful
For life, and for having traveled so far.

Acknowledgments

Having written these poems over a span of nearly twenty years, the reader will discover that there is no singular theme that emerges. Rather, I decided to place the poems as they were written—as expression ranging across a life's landscape that is at once personal, literary, domestic, sexual, theological, humorous, and observational. Indeed, wholly ordinary.

    I would like to thank those editors who have offered space in their respective publications for these varied poems.

Aperion Review: Sexual vs. Sensual, Seven Ways of Looking at a Nude Woman

Five Poetry: Venice in the Rain, Art in Florence, Homecoming, Singing the Blues

Indiana Voice Journal: Class Photos, Antiques, A Tree the Memory of a Tree, Passenger Pigeons

MM: Pandemic Prayer

Plough: The Kinship of Ordinary Things

The Lyric: In Paris, Mona Lisa in the Louvre, Anemone, Plurals

The Road Not Taken: Young Love & Old Love

Tribal Council (Indiana): Waapaahsiki Siipiiwi Mound

Additional poems were previously published in the chapbook, *Description by the Blind* (Tuckpoint Press, 2016).

About the Author

Todd Outcalt is the author of forty books in six languages, including the poetry collection, *Where in the World We Meet* (Chatter House Press) and the chapbook, *Description by the Blind and other poems* (Tuckpoint Press). His many other titles include *Common Ground* (Skyhorse), *Candles in the Dark* (John Wiley & Sons), *Blue Christmas* (Upper Room), and *Indiana Wineries* (Blue River). He has written for many magazines and also writes mystery and romance novels under his nom de plume, R. L. Perry. He lives in Brownsburg, Indiana and South Haven, Michigan with his wife and enjoys travel, hiking, painting, and kayaking.

www.ingramcontent.com/pod-product-compliance
Lightning Source LLC
Chambersburg PA
CBHW061458040426
42450CB00008B/1406